She Persisted

....

OPAL LEE

....

—INSPIRED BY—

She Persisted

by Chelsea Clinton & Alexandra Boiger

. . . .

OPAL
LEE

. . . .

written by
Shelia P. Moses

interior illustrations by
Gillian Flint

PHILOMEL

PHILOMEL
An imprint of Penguin Random House LLC, New York

First published in the United States of America by Philomel,
an imprint of Penguin Random House LLC, 2023

Visit us online at PenguinRandomHouse.com.

Library of Congress Cataloging-in-Publication Data is available.

HC ISBN 9780593623503
PB ISBN 9780593623510

1st Printing

Printed in the United States of America

LSCC

Edited by Talia Benamy.
Design by Ellice M. Lee.
Text set in LTC Kennerley Pro.

This book is for my mother,
Maless Moses. The world could bend you, Ma,
but it could not break you! You persisted!

DEAR READER,

As Sally Ride and Marian Wright Edelman both powerfully said, "You can't be what you can't see." When Sally said that, she meant that it was hard to dream of being an astronaut, like she was, or a doctor or an athlete or anything at all if you didn't see someone like you who already had lived that dream. She especially was talking about seeing women in jobs that historically were held by men.

I wrote the first *She Persisted* and the books that came after it because I wanted young girls—and children of all genders—to see women who worked hard to live their dreams. And I wanted all of us to see examples of persistence in the face of different challenges to help inspire us in our own lives.

I'm so thrilled now to partner with a sisterhood of writers to bring longer, more in-depth versions of these stories of women's persistence and achievement to readers. I hope you enjoy these chapter books as much as I do and find them inspiring and empowering.

And remember: If anyone ever tells you no, if anyone ever says your voice isn't important or your dreams are too big, remember these women. They persisted and so should you.

Warmly,

Chelsea Clinton

She Persisted

She Persisted: DEB HAALAND

She Persisted: BETHANY HAMILTON

She Persisted: DOROTHY HEIGHT

She Persisted: DOLORES HUERTA

She Persisted: FLORENCE GRIFFITH JOYNER

She Persisted: HELEN KELLER

She Persisted: CORETTA SCOTT KING

She Persisted: OPAL LEE

She Persisted: CLARA LEMLICH

She Persisted: RACHEL LEVINE

She Persisted: MAYA LIN

She Persisted: WANGARI MAATHAI

She Persisted: WILMA MANKILLER

She Persisted: PATSY MINK

She Persisted: FLORENCE NIGHTINGALE

She Persisted: NAOMI OSAKA

She Persisted: SALLY RIDE

She Persisted: MARGARET CHASE SMITH

She Persisted: SONIA SOTOMAYOR

She Persisted: MARIA TALLCHIEF

She Persisted: DIANA TAURASI

She Persisted: HARRIET TUBMAN

She Persisted: OPRAH WINFREY

She Persisted: MALALA YOUSAFZAI

OPAL
LEE

TABLE OF CONTENTS

....

Early Years

The name Opal means "precious stone" in Sanskrit. It is also the name of a specific type of stone, one that represents truth, purity, and hope. That made it a perfect name for Opal Flake. She was a fearless child who everyone knew was smart and helpful to those around her. After white people burned down her family home on June 19, 1939, little Opal knew that somehow one day, she would do something to make the world a better place. She also knew that June 19 was more than just an ordinary day.

Born in Marshall, Texas, on October 7, 1926, Opal was the firstborn of Otis Flake Sr. and Mattie Flake. The next year, Opal's little sister, Mary Elizabeth, came into the world, but she sadly died at only six months old. Soon her two brothers, Otis Jr. and Hugh, arrived, and Opal took her job as their big sister very seriously.

Life was not easy for Black families in Marshall, but the Flake household was full of love, even as Opal's parents worked hard each day. Opal and her brothers attended a segregated school, because everything was divided by race in most of Texas. The white children and Black children could not go to school together, play together, or even swim in the same pool. Opal

knew it was wrong, but she was a young Black

girl and there was nothing she could do about it.

Opal and her family were all so happy when

they moved into a new home in Marshall, behind

Wiley College, around 1932. It was not just any home, but a house her father had built with his own two hands. Sadly, a fire broke out at their new home the next year. No one was quite sure how that fire in 1933 got started, but after it was done, the home they loved was gone.

After the fire, the family struggled to rebuild. In 1937, they decided to move 185 miles away from Marshall to Fort Worth, Texas. They couldn't afford to buy or rent a house, so they lived with relatives until they could move out on their own. Mattie worked as a house cleaner and started making pies and selling them to the people in the neighborhood to earn extra money. Opal was proud that people loved her mother's food and called her mom the "Pie Lady."

The Flakes had a lot of family in Fort Worth,

and Opal enjoyed playing with her cousins and new friends. Just like in Marshall, though, everything in Fort Worth was segregated, so her playmates were all Black kids like her. Ten-year-old Opal and her little brothers attended the Copper School for six weeks before the family moved again. The children would have to find new friends in their new neighborhood and at school. Opal started attending a new school, where she settled into her classes.

Opal's parents didn't have a car, so every morning her mother and father went up the front steps of the bus, paid their bus fare, and got off the bus. Then they walked to the back of the bus and entered through the rear door to sit in the "colored section."

In 1938, Mattie fell on the bus, and she was

hurt. The city paid her for the accident, and her family used the money for a down payment on a new house. It was 1939 when the Flakes moved into their new home. Opal was sad to move again but happy they finally had a home of their own just like back in Marshall.

They were not there long before they realized they were not wanted in the mostly white neighborhood. On the morning of June 19, 1939, twelve-year-old Opal and her family looked outside and noticed a large crowd of white people gathered in their yard. Otis Sr. was at work, but he rushed home after someone went to his job and told him what was happening. He grabbed his shotgun and ran outside. The police did nothing to protect his family. "If you bust a cap, we'll let the mob have you," the police officers told him. Opal's dad was helpless as the crowd moved closer to his house. Otis Sr. put Opal and her little brothers in the hands of a neighbor who rushed them to a friend's house on nearby Terrell Avenue, where more Black families lived, away from the white neighborhood.

By nightfall, Opal's mother and father had gathered some of their belongings and also run from their home to safety. The white mob then made their way inside and started tearing up their furniture and throwing it outside. From where they had moved to safety, they could still see their house, and Opal and her family stood and watched their house burn to the ground. It was the second time this had happened to them.

The next year, the Flakes purchased a new home on Terrell Avenue and tried to put their

lives back together. But hard times and fear had broken Opal's mother and father's marriage apart. They divorced in 1942.

Opal was sixteen now, and she knew she had to be strong and helpful for her mother and little brothers. She kept making good grades and told her mother she was going to be a schoolteacher one day. Her future was bright.

································

Growing Up Fast

Opal was very proud when she entered I.M. Terrell High School, because it was the first Black high school in Fort Worth. She was proud to attend this historic school. Opal loved school, and she started telling her mother how she planned to return to Marshall to attend Wiley College. That way she could make her dream of being a teacher come true.

By her junior year of high school, though,

Opal had a boyfriend. He was a senior named Joe Roland, and when Opal started dating him, she stopped talking about going to college.

Days after graduating from high school in 1943, Opal announced that she was getting married. Mattie was so upset that her daughter was giving up on her college dreams that she did not even attend the wedding. But Opal was determined. She packed her bags and left to go start her new life.

Joe and Opal settled in as husband and wife. Times were hard for the young family, and instead of being a teacher, Opal found herself working long hours as a restroom attendant. She had to help Joe pay their rent at Butler Place, a public housing project. Housing projects were common for Black families in Fort Worth back then. The houses and apartments were owned by the government and the rent was very low.

Opal and Joe's marriage lasted only four years. During that time, Opal gave birth to four children. In 1947, Opal decided she was getting a divorce, like her mom and dad had. Her youngest child was only one month old when Opal knocked on her mother's door. She had no other place to go, but she knew she could go home. Mattie welcomed her daughter and grandchildren with open arms.

"I want to go to college, Mama," Opal told her mother in between tears. Not only did Mattie welcome Opal home, but she also told her she would babysit so that Opal could work toward her goals. Opal's dream was back on track, and Mattie was happy to help make it happen.

Within months, Opal was enrolled at Wiley College back in Marshall. During the week, she lived on campus, worked at the bookstore, and cleaned her cousin's house for extra money. Every Friday, she went back to Fort Worth to be with her family. On weekend nights, the young mother of four continued to work as a powder room atten- dant. For three and a half years, Opal traveled back and forth between Marshall and Fort Worth because she was determined to become a teacher. She was determined to provide a better life for herself and her children.

After finishing her courses, Opal had to complete her practice teaching, when new teach- ers would work in a classroom for one semester with an experienced teacher. Opal went to her professor and begged him to let her do her practice teaching in Fort Worth. Her professor said yes, and finally Opal was back at home with her children full-time.

Her children were getting older, and Opal needed more money to take care of them. Their father was not helping her very much, so she got a night job at a company that made airplanes. Convair was a big company, but the only job they had available for her was as a maid. She cleaned the restrooms at night and did her practice teaching during the day. This was very difficult, but she pressed on. Opal was determined not only to provide for her children but to help her mother financially. Mattie had taken care of the family for years, and Opal wanted her mother to know that she loved and appreciated her.

Opal was so proud that she had kept her promise to herself and to her mother. She was finally getting her college degree. At a time when most Black people didn't go to college, Opal received her bachelor's degree in education with a minor in English. Opal's mother and siblings were filled with joy. Graduation day was just the beginning of special moments and the family being proud of their Opal.

CHAPTER 3

The Educator

After graduation, Opal quickly found a job teaching third grade. She was not there long before she transferred to the elementary school she had attended as a child. What had then been called the Copper School was now Amanda McCoy School, and Opal loved teaching there. She understood the Black children in her neighborhood. Their needs were the same as hers had been when she was a child.

No matter how much she loved teaching, though, Opal still wasn't making enough money to care for her four children. She didn't have a car, so she rode to school each day with another teacher from McCoy. After school, her friend would pick her up and give her a ride to Convair, where she would work as a maid until midnight. For a few years Opal had worked both jobs to make ends meet. Eventually, Convair let a lot of their employees go, and Opal lost her night job.

At that point, Opal was still not earning all that much as a teacher, and she knew being laid off from Convair meant she would have to find extra work. Luckily, she did, landing a part-time job as editor of a small Black newspaper. There, she wrote stories about people of color for her community to read.

The newspaper job was perfect for Opal! Between her two jobs, she got to use her teaching skills to help children and her English skills to write and educate her community. She poured lessons about the history of America into her students and took pride in teaching her Black students about Black history that was not in their books. Both jobs made her happy. And she was even happier that she was able to provide a better life for her children.

As time went on, a lot changed at Amanda McCoy School. Opal was no longer just teaching Black children, but white and Mexican children, too. She loved being able to teach all of those kids. And change was happening in her life outside of school as well. Opal had fallen in love again, and in 1967, she married Dale T. Lee. He was a principal at a school in Fort Worth. Life was finally falling into place for Opal.

After a few years, Opal stopped teaching in the classroom and became a visiting teacher. As a visiting teacher, she was required to go to the homes of students when there was a problem. This mainly happened when students missed school a lot, and it was a visiting teacher's job to find out what was going on. Opal quickly learned that there were many reasons why students were missing school. Some of the children or their parents had medical problems, others didn't have enough food to eat, and some didn't have clothes to wear to school. Opal was sad to find out that some of the children were even homeless.

When she had been teaching in a classroom, Opal knew that some of her students faced problems, but nothing had prepared her for major issues like this. With each case, Opal would spring into action to help the parents and the children. She would often go to the food bank and deliver food to the families. She was brokenhearted to see all the families in line each day at the food banks, and she was determined to help them.

The situation was so bad that Opal wound up needing assistance with the hundreds of cases she was assigned. She decided to go to the superintendent, the person in charge of all the schools in that area, to tell him she needed help. He responded, "If you can't do the job, I will find someone else." Opal was shocked, but she was not discouraged. She persisted, working hard to keep on meeting the needs of the children. She was not going to let the children down! Never!

....

CHAPTER 4

The Activist

Opal and Dale both retired in 1977, but Opal's work to help her students and their parents was far from over. She could not forget about all the students who were missing school because they didn't have clothes to wear. And the thought of just one child going to bed hungry brought tears to her eyes.

While working as a visiting teacher, Opal had become a regular at the food bank, so it was

a perfect place to become a volunteer after retire-
ment. She found herself helping families there
daily, and she eventually took on a bigger leadership role and became a board member. As a board

member, Opal worked hard to make sure no one in the community was hungry. But the food bank itself had problems. The physical condition of the building was not good. The food bank also had broken refrigerators, and sometimes the food was not fresh. People complained, and the CEO in charge of the whole food bank was called to Dallas to meet with the attorney general, the government official responsible for monitoring all the state's food banks. Eventually, Opal was put in charge of making the food bank a better place for the community she loved dearly.

Then, tragedy struck! Someone torched the building, and it went up in flames. Opal and the others who worked there were shocked and horrified. Just like the two fires that had destroyed her houses when she was a girl, the food bank burning down was heartbreaking. Opal and her co-workers wondered whether the fire might not really have been an accident, but they had no proof of who started the fire or why.

Opal insisted that they focus on the people they needed to serve. Fire or no fire, building or no building, they knew they could not let people in Fort Worth go hungry. Not to be defeated, they rented an abandoned guacamole factory in Opal's neighborhood. It cost a lot, but they were able to use the insurance money from the fire to pay the monthly bills. The larger space gave them more room for refrigerators, which meant more fresh items and frozen food for the people they served.

A year went by, and the food bank was better than ever with a mostly new staff, volunteers, and board members. One day, when Opal was in

her office, the owner of the building showed up.

"It looks like you are doing a good job of feeding families, so we are giving you the building," he said. Opal was so happy! Their hard work, persistence during difficult times, and prayers had paid off.

As the years passed, Opal retired from the board, and one of the local churches took over operation of the food bank. She stopped going to the food bank daily, but anytime she was told a family was in need and didn't have transportation, Opal would pick up the food and make a special delivery.

She still dreamed of a world where food banks were no longer needed, but until then, she continued the work that had to be done. In many ways, Opal's commitment to others had just begun.

CHAPTER 5

Juneteenth

Throughout the time that Opal lived in Fort Worth, both as a teacher and as a volunteer at the food bank, she witnessed poverty and injustice in the state of Texas. And she didn't just witness it—she lived it herself, and she understood the history and the struggle of people of color in that state. She had watched her family's house being burned down on June 19 so many years ago, and she knew that the date was important for other reasons as well.

For many years, Opal had taught her students about the history of Black people in Texas. Part of that history included what happened there on June 19, 1865. Opal always made sure to teach her classes about that day, but outside of Texas, few people knew about it. It was a day that became known as Juneteenth.

The story of Juneteenth went back to the time of the Civil War, when the Union in the North and the Confederacy in the South had fought over whether to end the terrible system of slavery in the United States. Although President Abraham Lincoln issued the Emancipation Proclamation and freed all enslaved people in the Southern states on January 1, 1863, there were many still living in Galveston, Texas. They were not actually freed because they were still under Confederate control—and many of them didn't even know that they were supposed to have been freed. Their masters continued to keep them enslaved to work in their fields, clean their houses, and take care of their children. Some of them were even still sold to other plantation owners, who were also keeping the secret of their freedom.

All of this changed when a Union general named Gordon Granger, along with a few thousand mostly Black Union troops, arrived in Galveston. That was the day General Granger stood in front of what's now Reedy Chapel AME Church and brought news of General Order No. 3.

It said: "The people are informed that, in accordance with a proclamation from the Executive of the United States, all slaves are free."

Most of the enslaved people in Galveston were still in the fields, so they didn't know what had happened until later that day. Many of them couldn't read or write, but the message got passed along by word of mouth. When they were told, they cheered and celebrated. People who had been enslaved their entire lives were enslaved no more. They were in disbelief. They were all free! And since the enslaved people in Galveston were the last ones in the country to be told about their freedom, the day turned into a holi-day 156 years later.

General Order No. 3 indeed notified those enslaved of their freedom, but it also asked them to stay in Texas to work for low wages. Most of them ignored the request and left on foot to live as free people. So many of their family members had been sold, and they wanted to try to find them.

The following year on June 19, those who had been freed and remained in Galveston celebrated what they referred to as Jubilee Day with food and music. They even created a red drink out of strawberries and lemonade. The red represented the suffering of slavery.

Over the years, Jubilee Day became known as Juneteenth. Parades were added to the celebrations, along with church services and parties for everyone. It became a family affair for Opal, her children, and families across Texas. Opal knew that Juneteenth was more than a celebration, and she wanted to make sure that Black people for generations to come learned what had happened to their ancestors. She wanted people who were not descendants of slaves to know, too.

Opal said, "I try to get people to understand it's not a Texas thing, is not a Black thing—it's freedom for everybody." People need to know what happened, she insisted.

Opal was determined to spread the word about Juneteenth—and about the celebration of freedom that it stood for. And she had been doing that work for years. In 1977, Opal became a founding member of the Tarrant County Black Historical and Genealogical Society, a group that was started by Ms. Lenora Rolla. Its mission was to record and preserve the history of Black people in Fort Worth and throughout Texas. The very first year it was formed, Opal was assigned to organize a Juneteenth celebration in Fort Worth.

There had already been a group of well-meaning people raising money and hosting a small Juneteenth celebration for years. Opal and the newly formed society soon became in charge of running the event. Under Opal's leadership and with much excitement from the community, the Juneteenth celebration became a bigger yearly event.

Just like the enslaved people did when they learned of their freedom in 1865, the Black community in Fort Worth celebrated each year by dancing and singing in the streets, and with lots of food for the community. Under Opal's watch, the Juneteenth celebration grew larger and larger as time went on, bringing the community together.

Opal and other Fort Worth residents enjoyed the annual event, but they knew that it was more than just a party—it was also a teaching tool. During the celebration, they spoke to people about what Juneteenth meant. They also gave out flyers and held workshops to teach the young and the old what had happened in Galveston the century before they were born.

Opal had loved her journey as a teacher and a volunteer at the food bank, and as she did those things, she also felt strongly about this mission. It was a mission to spread her knowledge about the importance of Juneteenth to the country and to the world.

The Long Walk

With that mission in mind, Opal and other Texans began talking about making Juneteenth an official state holiday. They wrote letters to politicians and would not take no for an answer. In 1979, a member of the Texas House of Representatives named Albert Ely Edwards worked to make a law in the state that would do just that. It passed, and Juneteenth was declared a state holiday in Texas the following year!

Juneteenth would be celebrated as an official holiday for the first time in Texas in 1980. Opal and her friends might have been happy with just that, but they knew it was only the beginning.

State after state followed in the steps of Texas to make Juneteenth a state holiday, with a lot of hard work from people who knew how important it was. At the same time, a new movement was brewing, and Opal was front and center. People wanted Juneteenth to become a national holiday. It was important to them that this historic day receive the full recognition and honor it deserved.

In the early nineties, Opal decided to join the National Juneteenth Observance Foundation, an organization whose goal was to make Juneteenth a national holiday. As a board member, she worked closely with the founder, Reverend Ronald V. Myers Sr. His passion and hard work had helped encourage forty-six states, plus Washington, DC, to declare Juneteenth as a state holiday or day of observance. They wanted to do the same for the country as a whole, not just for individual states, and they all knew they could get it done, even if it meant a lot more hard work. In 1994, Opal made the journey to New Orleans to meet with Rev. Myers and other members of the foundation as they laid out the groundwork for what is now known as the Modern Juneteenth Movement.

Making Juneteenth a national holiday was not going to be easy. As time went by, many gave up, but not Rev. Myers and Opal. Even after Rev. Myers died, Opal's journey continued. She knew it could be done, but how?

In her eighties now, Opal had been fighting for years, and in 2008, she thought she had found her path forward. Barack Obama was running for president, and if he won, he would become the first Black president the United States had ever had. *Surely*, she thought, *Juneteenth will become a national holiday if Obama is elected.* So when Opal heard that Obama was going to be in Dallas, she was determined to meet him. With two of her friends pushing her in a wheelchair, Opal made her way to Obama to tell him her vision. *The Dallas Morning News* snapped a picture of Obama and Opal that spread across the state.

After Obama was elected as the forty-fourth president of the United States, Opal began her letter-writing campaign to him and First Lady Michelle Obama. For eight years she wrote letters to both requesting a meeting. For eight years she asked the same question: "Do you know that Juneteenth is a state holiday in forty-five states?" She asked the first lady to please tell the president that she would like him to declare Juneteenth a national holiday.

Opal continued to press President Obama and other leaders for years, but Juneteenth still had not become a national holiday. In 2016, at the age of eighty-nine, Opal knew she had to try something else. She thought back on the history of the Civil Rights Movement, which fought for equal rights for Black people in the US. That movement had organized marches in Birmingham, Alabama, Albany, Georgia, and other places in the South all the way to Washington, DC, to raise their voices and call attention to their cause. Opal knew that she could make her own version of a march and raise her own voice for the cause along the way.

Her goal was not to march 1,600 miles from Texas to Washington, DC, all at once, but to go to different cities across the country and march two and a half miles in each city, with the final march in the capital. Opal hadn't just chosen two and a half miles randomly—the distance was meant to represent the two and a half years that enslaved people in Galveston had been held in bondage after the Emancipation Proclamation was issued. She knew she had to send a message with her marches, and that was a big part of it.

Surrounded by family and friends, Opal's journey started at Baker Chapel African Methodist Episcopal Church in Fort Worth. Would she be able to walk the distance? She put her mind to it

and began, and two and a half miles later, Opal arrived in Joppa, Texas. She had made it!

This was just the beginning of Opal's journey, which took her through Texas, Michigan, Nevada, and other states as she repeated the two-and-a-half-mile walks. In 2017, she finally reached Washington, DC.

Though President Obama was no longer in office, Opal's drive to make Juneteenth a national holiday continued. She had lived through fourteen presidents. When Opal was born, Calvin Coolidge had been president of the United States. When she started pushing for a state holiday in 1979, Jimmy Carter was president. She had lived long enough to see a Black man become president, and for that, she was grateful. But for all she had lived to see, she still hadn't seen Juneteenth made into a national holiday. Opal knew there was more still to be done.

So in 2019, when Opal was ninety-two years old, she put on her walking shoes once again. And this time, she did even more. In addition to traveling from state to state for her two-and-a-half-mile walks, she started a campaign to gather one million signatures to submit to Congress, each one supporting the idea of making Juneteenth a national holiday. She wanted to show just how many people agreed with her and her mission. And she worked with Congresswoman Sheila Jackson Lee to write a law in Congress that would make the holiday official nationwide. Opal was more determined than ever to get it done.

Even during the COVID-19 pandemic, Opal Lee kept on marching and making calls to the

White House and to members of Congress. When people learned what city Opal was traveling to, they would join her as she marched. These marches together became known as Opal's Walk. She also kept collecting signatures to send to Congress, still aiming to get a million of them, and young people around the country joined in that effort.

Then a huge moment arrived. Producer and rap icon Sean "Diddy" Combs joined Opal on social media to tell her that she had reached one million signatures. She screamed with laughter, and the word spread. Within days, they were up to 1.5 million signatures, a number that US politicians couldn't possibly ignore. Opal and those fighting alongside her had done it.

On June 17, 2021, forty-four years after she had hosted her first Juneteenth celebration in

Texas, Opal Lee walked into the White House and stood next to the desk of President Joe Biden. Congresswoman Sheila Jackson Lee, her champion in Congress, stood by her side as President Biden signed the Juneteenth National Independence Day Act into law. Juneteenth was now a federal holiday.

The next day, people who had never even heard of Juneteenth were chatting about the new federal holiday. They were not only celebrating Juneteenth being a holiday, but they were also celebrating Opal Lee.

Opal Lee has survived more in her lifetime than one person should have to endure. She was a teen bride and a maid before becoming an educator, activist, and leader. She worked to feed the hungry, and even started a farm in Fort Worth to

help more people find ways to eat and be healthy.

Opal watched her family home burn down on June 19, 1939, and eighty-two years later she witnessed that day become a national day for freedom. She showed us all how to persist!

HOW YOU CAN PERSIST

By Shelia P. Moses

Do you want to serve others and help celebrate history like Opal Lee? Here are some ways you can help your community and the world.

1. Never give up. Opal went back to college while caring for four little children with her mother's help. She pushed for better conditions at the food bank and made it happen. And she worked hard to celebrate

Black history and share its importance with all Americans. Her persistence throughout her life resulted in Juneteenth becoming a national holiday. You can also push hard for the things you care about.

2. Share your knowledge with others, especially about your own culture and heritage.

3. There are Juneteenth celebrations around the country now. Attend the parades and workshops, and visit Black history museums on Juneteenth and throughout the year.

4. There are books about Juneteenth for both young people and adults. Read books to teach yourself and others what Juneteenth really means. Give your friends and family

books about this historic holiday.

5. Opal is known for her work related to Juneteenth, but she is also known for her kind spirit and love for young people. Remember to be kind to others with your words and deeds.

6. If you see something that is wrong, say something! Opal saw so much injustice as a child. She fought her entire life for equality for all people. You can do the same. If you see someone mistreating a friend or classmate, let an adult know.

7. You don't have to have a lot of money to give. Opal helped so many people while working at the food bank. Give your time to someone who is alone. Show them that you care.

ACKNOWLEDGMENTS

I now divide my life's journey personally and professionally into two parts. Life before stage 3 breast cancer and life after being diagnosed. In my life before breast cancer, I was writing about the brave men and women who came before me. In my life afterward, I am still writing about those people. One of the sheroes at the top of my list before cancer was Ms. Opal Lee. Although the project was delayed, it was not denied. And just like that, publishers Jill Santopolo and Talia Benamy contacted me to tell her story years later.

What a confirmation that my life before cancer had been restored. Thank you, Talia and Jill! Your editorial skills made this journey to tell Ms. Opal Lee's story a beautiful walk in the park. What a great honor to be a member of the "Persisterhood."

Thank you, Chelsea Clinton, for this brilliant concept to help young women of all colors and backgrounds understand who they are and how they too must persist.

Thank you to my biological sisters and my sister-friends, who remind me daily that we really do make the world go around. And last but never least, Ma! You persisted!

❦ References ❧

Carmel, Julia. "Opal Lee's Juneteenth Vision
Is Becoming Reality." *The New York Times*,
June 18, 2021.

Fox 4 Staff. "Opal Lee, Grandmother of
Juneteenth, Celebrates Birthday with Day
of Service." October 8, 2022. fox4news.com
/news/opal-lee-juneteenth-day-of-service.

Jewel, Kirsti. *What Is Juneteenth?* New York:
Penguin Random House, 2022.

Lee, Opal. *Juneteenth: A Children's Story*. Fort
Worth, TX: Unity Unlimited, 2021.

Norwood, Arlisha. *The History of Juneteenth: A History Book for New Readers.* Oakland, CA: Rockridge Press, 2022.

Womack Howard, Renetta T. *Opal's Walk: The Life and Works of Opal Flake Roland Lee.* Renetta T. Womack Howard, 2020.

SHELIA P. MOSES is a poet, playwright, novelist, and historian. In the last three decades, she has authored numerous books for children, young adults, and adults, including Dick Gregory's memoir, *Callus on My Soul*. Her young adult classic, *The Legend of Buddy Bush*, was nominated for a National Book Award and named a Coretta Scott King Honor Book. In 2009, Shelia's novel *Joseph* was nominated for the NAACP Image Award. She was thrilled when her play, *I, Dred Scott*, adapted from the book, was showcased at the Missouri History Museum. In 2018, she started a project to place a little free library in every township in her native county of Northampton, North Carolina. They now have ten libraries. She is also the founder of the George Moses Horton Book Festival. Shelia lives in Old Town, Alexandria, Virginia.

Courtesy of the author

You can visit Shelia P. Moses online at
SheliaPMoses.com
and follow her on Twitter
@SheliaPMoses

GILLIAN FLINT has worked as a professional illustrator since earning an animation and illustration degree in 2003. Her work has since been published in the UK, USA and Australia. In her spare time, Gillian enjoys reading, spending time with her family and puttering about in the garden on sunny days. She lives in the northwest of England.

You can visit Gillian Flint online at
gillianflint.com
or follow her on Instagram
@gillianflint_illustration

CHELSEA CLINTON is the author of the #1 *New York Times* bestseller *She Persisted: 13 American Women Who Changed the World*; *She Persisted Around the World: 13 Women Who Changed History*; *She Persisted in Sports: American Olympians Who Changed the Game*; *She Persisted in Science: Brilliant Women Who Made a Difference*; *Don't Let Them Disappear: 12 Endangered Species Across the Globe*; *Welcome to the Big Kids Club*; *It's Your World: Get Informed, Get Inspired & Get Going!*; *Start Now!: You Can Make a Difference*; with Hillary Clinton, *Grandma's Gardens* and *Gutsy Women*; and, with Devi Sridhar, *Governing Global Health: Who Runs the World and Why?* She is also the Vice Chair of the Clinton Foundation, where she works on many initiatives, including those that help empower the next generation of leaders. She lives in New York City with her husband, Marc, and their children.

You can follow Chelsea Clinton on Twitter
@ChelseaClinton
or on Facebook at
facebook.com/chelseaclinton

ALEXANDRA BOIGER has illustrated nearly twenty picture books, including the She Persisted books by Chelsea Clinton; the popular Tallulah series by Marilyn Singer; and the Max and Marla books, which she also wrote. Originally from Munich, Germany, she now lives outside of San Francisco, California, with her husband, Andrea, daughter, Vanessa, and two cats, Luiso and Winter.

You can visit Alexandra Boiger online at
alexandraboiger.com
or follow her on Instagram
@alexandra_boiger

Read about more inspiring women in the

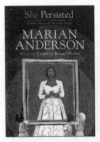

She Persisted series!

She Persisted

NELLIE BLY

Written by Michelle Knudsen

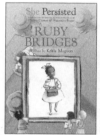

She Persisted

RUBY BRIDGES

Written by Kekla Magoon

She Persisted

KALPANA CHAWLA

Written by Raakhee Mirchandani

She Persisted

CLAUDETTE COLVIN

Written by Lesa Cline-Ransome

She Persisted

BETHANY HAMILTON

Written by Maryann Cocca-Leffler

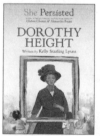

She Persisted

DOROTHY HEIGHT

Written by Kelly Starling Lyons

She Persisted

DOLORES HUERTA

Written by Monica Brown

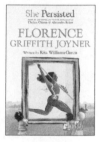

She Persisted

FLORENCE GRIFFITH JOYNER

Written by Rita Williams-Garcia

She Persisted

RACHEL LEVINE

Written by Lisa Bunker

She Persisted

MAYA LIN

Written by Grace Lin

She Persisted

WANGARI MAATHAI

Written by Eucabeth Odhiambo

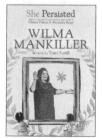

She Persisted

WILMA MANKILLER

Written by Traci Sorell

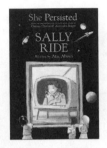

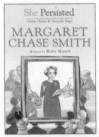